So the Sadness Could Not Hurt

So the Sadness Could Not Hurt

Poems by

Ruth Towne

© 2025 Ruth Towne. All rights reserved.
This material may not be reproduced in any form, published,
reprinted, recorded, performed, broadcast,
rewritten, or redistributed without
the explicit permission of Ruth Towne.
All such actions are strictly prohibited by law.

Cover design by Shay Culligan
Cover image by Courtney Hill on Unsplash
Author photo by Sarah La Croix Photography

ISBN: 978-1-63980-678-2

Kelsay Books
502 South 1040 East, A-119
American Fork, Utah 84003
Kelsaybooks.com

Acknowledgments

Many thanks to the editors of the following publications where these poems first appeared, sometimes in alternate versions:

Beyond Words Literary Magazine: "Clotho, Lachesis, Atropos"
Black Spot Books: "Better Homes and Gardens"
Coalition for Digital Narratives: "From Boughs," "Subject / Object," "Thresholds: Maple Street, February"
Coffin Bell Journal: "Death, a Hall of Mirrors"
The Decadent Review: "Return to Sender"
Drunk Monkeys: "To Grow, for My Grandfather"
Ghost City Review: "Deer Receive the Ash"
Grim & Gilded: "Open Graves in Spring"
Inlandia Publishing: "A Question to the Tea Leaves," "Sum," "Dishes by Hand," "Parable at the Office," "My Holy Poltergeist"
Mantis: "Leap," "Torricelli Apparatus"
miniMAG: "9:00 A.M., Sanctuary," "Next Left"
Moot Point Magazine: "Mother Murders Marion Crane"
New Feathers Anthology: "Composite Reconstruction"
NiftyLit: "Creation of Eve / Sleep of Adam"
Orange Juice: "Sweets to the Sweet"
The Orchards Poetry Journal: "So the Sadness Could Not Hurt"
Plainsongs Magazine: "Situation Comedy"
Poet's Choice: "Woman, Wellside"
Sad Girl Diaries: "Sunlight Through the Center Street Window"
Voices Literary Project: "A Family Portrait"
Wingless Dreamer Magazine: "View from Highway 46"
Z Publication House, Best Emerging Poets Series: "Compass," "Heraldic Display," "Head of a Woman," "Composite Magdalene," "Kite Over Moody Beach," "Follow Out the Happiest Story"

Contents

9:00 A.M., Sanctuary	11
Sunlight Through the Center Street Window	12
My Holy Poltergeist	13
Deer Receive the Ash	15
Heraldic Display, Ancestry	16
Next Left, the Numinous	19
Parable at the Office	20
Composite Reconstruction	21
Sweets to the Sweet	23
Torricelli Apparatus	24
Kite Over Moody Beach	26
A Question to the Tea Leaves	27
To Grow, for My Grandfather	28
Composite Magdalene	30
Compass	31
Follow Out the Happiest Story	32
Creation of Eve / Sleep of Adam	33
View from Highway 46	34
Situation Comedy	36
A Family Portrait, or From Daughter to Father	37
From Boughs	38
Thresholds: Maple Street, February	39
Return to Sender	40
Leap	41
Dishes by Hand, Sleight of Hand	43
Woman, Wellside	44
Head of a Woman	45
Mother Murders Marion Crane	46
Open Graves in Spring	48
Subject / Object	49
Clotho, Lachesis, Atropos	50
Better Homes and Gardens	51
Sum	52
Death, a Hall of Mirrors	53
So the Sadness Could Not Hurt	54

9:00 A.M., Sanctuary

I pray for a name
someone else
has written

on a red balloon
in black marker.

Now balloons rise
toward the rafters.

I'd rather release
mine outside.

What could stop
my prayer then?

A contrail unwinds
behind an aircraft.

The unbound
thought escapes
as a prayer,

persists in the rafters
in effigy of worship.

Sunlight Through the Center Street Window

You said, *This is a girl's apartment,* as plaits of sunshine
swayed on the pressed and white shoulders of our walls,
as sunlight brushed three pairs of jade succulents poised
like pearl-strings against a sun-starched collarbone.

Beside the sofa, light tangled the split ends of tea
candles where shine feathered at night. We sat
in the sun on the bamboo (I said, *wicker*) couch.
Now, the seat seems the color of honey, hardening

and dimming brunette. But it was only the usual milky
cushion turning the usual cream when warmed by the light.
And light combed the couch in our living room all day,
kept smoothing it down strand after strand.

When you swept, you said, *Hair—hair, everywhere.* And rain
did strike our windows. The sunlight accounted for only half
the story. Evenings, you took down the painting and its frame,
exchanged it for the dartboard, while the stovetop burned

with the rice. But even on those evenings, we sensed sunlight
in the bronze of warm apple cider. One night, you dreamed
you had harvested your gilded hair (you said, *I threshed
it smooth like straw*) and passed it to the landlord with the rent.

Then a week passed. We began to uproot ourselves, our plants,
collecting empty bedframes and blankets. When we gathered
our belongings, you realized we couldn't reap that sunlight.
And in the end, we painted the white walls goldenrod.

My Holy Poltergeist

First, at the front door, once, twice,
a third time before I let you in, Jesus,
before you made a home in the attic
of my soul. But that was years ago.

I remember you now on occasion,
though lately most every night
dancing to the rhythm of the water
pipes. Do you dream of leaving?

But the attic for you, you alone.
I keep you up there set apart.
You could say I keep you holy.
Remember, as your parable says,

I heard you knock, I let you in
so I could keep you in the attic
of my soul. I imagine you rest
during the day, next to the chest

where for so long my mother
kept her wedding dress. I'll save
a strand of Christmas lights next
year so you can read at night.

Again you knock, on the living
room wall this time. Any harder
and you'd have dropped the family
portrait off the clean white wall.

Jesus, don't you see? This is your attic,
No less than a cathedral in my soul.
Look, the rafters resemble the ribcage
of a sanctuary, and my storage boxes

make two rows of pews. Jesus, only
the finest for you. Yet you tap the walls,
my friendly ghost, my Jesus. I hear you
on the second floor. A door slams.

I hear you whisper. Speak louder,
please. If I search, would you come
down for me? Jesus, I never asked
before—would you find me if I admit

I need you? I need you. I need you
to call me to the attic where you stay,
call me back and lock me up. Dear
Jesus, save yourself some knocking.

Deer Receive the Ash

Lent arrives, and the deer fast
their own antlers. At dusk,
at dawn, they graze buds
of clover. Hollow honeycomb
dense as bone sops oxygen
and blood below the fabric skin.
But the antler is a false bone.

The deer, gentle as prayers
in the open field, drape
sackcloth across their faces,
velvet dry as ash.

Heraldic Display, Ancestry

The woman in the open casket
is not my great-grandmother,
but her daughter sees her hands

and so believes her by her hands.
Silence, a lie of kindness. The man
in a red coat tangled in sleigh bells

is not Saint Nick. Quick to trick
the eye, he evades the twinkle
lights so I cannot see my uncle.

My shape in the mirror is not
my mother's. The third Mark
in the family is not dead, only

moved away though the joke
says otherwise. The rooftop
shakes above my bed, snow

and ice slide past skylight,
but the sound I hear is not
reindeer but my father above

me jumping. The story I tell
is not my mother's. Tell me,
where is my great-grandmother

now? Distinct, intact, the family
line appears as far back in time
as Christ on earth, a deep crease

in the center of a palm, a life line
curves, a fate line folds. A mark
of my family—three named Mark:

my father's brother, their nephew,
my brother. Others: blue eyes,
freckles, and slender fingers

not unlike my great-grandmother's.
How many times has my mother
told me my body is not her body?

My grandmother believes the body
she sees. A great-grandfather of mine
died at sea, drowned, corpse not found.

A gun killed my father's brother,
a driver his sister, ancestral aunt
hanged front and center Salem.

Mark Howard Clark. Mark Howard
Jones. Mark Howard Clark II.
Now, bring me my matriarch's body,

great-mother a decade decayed.
I wear her jewels: a diamond
ring, a sapphire pin, and pearls

around which her bones curl
in the shape of her hand. Young,
my brothers and I would sing,

*Do Lord, oh do, Lord, oh do
remember me.* There's a man
on the roof, my father; a shadow,

my mother; and an empty space
prepares to take another brother.
I see my father see, in the face

of his second son, his brother,
long dead at sixteen or himself
younger than any grief. Together

the two brothers live in mine.
Iniquity of a father visits children
to the third and fourth generation.

When can I meet my Uncle Mark?
At my grandmother's funeral, I open
the casket to discover her mother.

Next Left, the Numinous

I must be walking in a narrow alley.
Light glows far to my left, my right,

never both sides at once. I'm lost,
it's night, and darkness amplifies,

obscures my sight. I imply by lack
of light my confusion, my questions

about life. I fear the Second Coming
and what evidence the Holy Spirit

has extracted from the crime scene
of my conscience, a strand of hair,

a speck of spit cast between the gap
in my front teeth. I walk all night,

arrive at no city. Iris commands
pupil to widen, a well wanting water.

Airglow of night, half-moon, or star—
some things remain hidden from sight,

an answer withheld, a silence to purify.
Bright heaven, where marquee lights

ever shine, why can't I find you?
Heaven, light up your neon sign.

Parable at the Office

for D.L., S.S., D.M., and J.L.

At work after the weekend, I replace office plants.
That they grow is my miracle, my loaves and fish.
On a windowsill three cubicles from mine, shines
the sunlight. My plants grow every five days, only

in the pair of days I am away. Five loaves, two fish.
Strangers in a crowd wish they were not famished,
but Jesus feeds them for a day. I refresh my plants,
slip and spill water on my monitor. I recall an article

about a warehouse where the workers live in shifts,
about workers whose complex convenience store shoe
store drug store is down the compound hall, workers
who share every eight hours a cot. It's clockwork,

their seamless transition. A timecard to work, to eat,
a timecard to bathe and to sleep. From assembly line
window, a worker flies to a net below, flops and flails
in open air. Security bag, ID, and timecard shine, scales

in second-shift sun. Pothos plant sticks to windowpane,
one green leaf remains on glass. So another parable:
the apostle Peter receives Caesar's dues in a trout's mouth.
Jesus grants many a fish, a timecard for you and for me.

Composite Reconstruction

I view the color first, one shade of yellow,
and another, A1 then C2, neither white.
Mine are teeth unbleached. The assistant
explains my teeth are dry, dehydrated.

The dentist promises a change in their shade
post-procedure. A question: C2—do you agree?
An answer: yes. The dentist addresses the front
tooth I chipped in two, to shape and make it new.

Dentist and assistant pass tools above my face.
I lay flat between them but cannot translate
these foreign objects. A board game, I receive
their action. Their tools, one planchette, slide

from side to side. I am their Ouija board.
They shape questions and record the vowels
I return until they restore my tooth. Overlarge,
imprecise, grotesque—where was nothing,

now a false tooth. Only vowels, the occasional *y*
possess me. Multiple choice: shape here, here,
here, or all of the above? He says shape, shaves
is what he means. The structure looms. An answer,

a guess, a yes to all. Their game resumes. A response
essay: I request a hairstylist trim around my face,
she asks where I like my bangs to fall, eyebrow
or eye? I save the risk for another day. Who am I

to say, yes, this is the shape I choose for my tooth?
After two hours, the dentist reviews his work,
requests feedback. I suggest perhaps more shaping.
He instructs me then to test it out, return for a trim

in about a week if I need. To choose a new tooth
is a lesson self-taught. I concede. A bonus point:
I imagine in place of my new tooth what the dentist
of one hundred years ago would have reclaimed,

a central incisor straight from a dead soldier's head.
This improves my mood, though slightly. My tongue
relearns my tooth, new and smooth. I will have always
possessed this tooth soon, but for now to speak, I lisp.

Sweets to the Sweet

In a far lane, a capped swimmer slaps
water, lap after lap, two cupped hands

clap in cavernous room, the steady
beat of a vena cava. I wade deeper

than my knees. Chlorine circumvents
the scent of lavender I used in a room

in a distant life. Three drips of herbal oil
to one drinking glass produces this—

memory of ammonia, chloramines trapped
in black nylon swimwear, against skin,

deep in damp hair. I wade here, past thigh
to hip until I begin to swim. How strange,

to fail the diving board leap and swimming
school, then to use the public pool to soothe

one's self. Slight the measure—one second
in a twelve-day span, one drop in eighteen

gallons—the scent of chlorine floods
my senses, water against me presses

on all sides. As I move, water smooths
me. I am the stones I carry. I reach out

for laps ever toward the deep end. Calm,
the deeper water I tread inside my mind.

Torricelli Apparatus

> *. . . and this is the wonder that's keeping the stars apart*
> —e. e. cummings, [i carry your heart with me (i carry it in)]

I am lonely soon, I imagine you are, too.
When we drive together you keep the radio
low to subdue the soundwaves, but we talk
anyway, supplementing the time lost away.

We linger though this is not the first or last
of our goodbyes, but the outer space of spatial
relationship. Later, your plane brings the dim sky
closer to itself, this slow rate over time. Absence

demands I fill your place, remains greedy
and unsatisfied. Consider outer space, a near
perfect vacuum in nature, so you say. Gaseous
pressure stages constellations, heavenly bodies

among waves of light. Stars parse darkness
before they score aircrafts' backs, bringing
some close, taking you far. You and I relate
to light and sound—both move in space as waves

or not at all, so our movement has its restrictions,
careful definition. Outer space validates our void
and vacant art. Our two bodies separate forget
touch, remember the fact of past pressure only.

I separate space, alternate distance and absence.
To remember is pressure unto itself. Light, sound
waves pass between us. A face onscreen, a voice
reaches me at lightspeed. My inner ear vibrates,

tries to find inside the sine waves your body,
strange search in the dark. Hot air from my long
breath reacts above where I cross your gravel
driveway, contracts, cools. I learned fast never

to look back to the doorway where last I saw you.
If I was lonely then, what now? I say, You mute
the radio so that I won't sing so loud. This truth
does not crush me, in the background still

music plays. Sound has no echo in space,
touch demands two objects. I sense another
absence. In my chest, radio waves vibrate.
I drive away from you and sing. Our distance

makes a strange way to be alone, a stranger way
to love—gives us both one atom of air per cubic
meter and says to each, partake, partake. We break,
communing in halves, separate until our vacuum

collapses at last. This event horizon, a vast black
hole, consumes all, even waves of sound and light.
Nature hates a vacuum, surrenders itself to create
from nothing, something, longs to satisfy the void.

Kite Over Moody Beach

The gesture of a diamond kite
high and deep over ocean mirrors

the motion of a side stroke—
when I give you the light blue

plastic spool, it fits your hand
as it does mine, only tighter.

The wind like a rip current
drags the kite out by fathoms,

or what I imagine as a fathom,
and you pursue by the string

the kite, run down the beach
with the sun on bare chest

and back. I call back to you.
The canvas dives nose first

at the surf. You turn. The sand
keeps you, a strong current of land.

The line slacks with it the kite.
I reach you moments after, stand

beside you on the beach, ankle deep.
The waves wind the halved canvas back,

tangle its twine. Above, seagulls mock
our paper crane while we are silent.

My love, withdraw our kite
from the water, ask it again to fly.

A Question to the Tea Leaves

In the teacup, only a teaspoon
of liquid remains, almost room
temperature now. My left hand
lifts the cup, my eyelids drop
for a moment. I sense but cannot
see the tea as I swirl it once,
twice, a third time counter
to the face of a clock. Eyes open.
The saucer collects what's left
as I invert its cup. A magpie outside
my kitchen window pries at my private
moment, then shakes its wings
toward the bright sky. The tea drains.
I wish for a basket of flowers. And it drains,
perhaps a second bird in an open cage, or
the magnolia, yes, I wish the magnolia
as it drains and it drains. It drains
and the leaves that remain
shape themselves into a harp.

To Grow, for My Grandfather

In my backyard, dandelions have assembled,
twelve pastel tribes. Together, their yellow
heads like piles of stones form springtime altars.
And they grow so because I have not mowed

my lawn. By and by the daylight journeys by,
adds another stone to praise the spring. An altar
says my grandfather, is a remembering thing,
what Moses built when he saw into Canaan,

the promised land, where honey and milk flowed,
and I know no one bothered him to cut the lawn.
In the front yard, I expected tiger lily blooms
where four or five clusters of wide-bladed grass

rise by the driveway. Now a single daffodil
stands at the edge of my grass and gravel.
Like that lonesome usher, my grandfather stooping
at the door of his church, it welcomes me across

the threshold onto the lawn. And the grass there
rises high and higher past my ankles to my knees
in praise of nimbus, of cirrus in the wild sanctuary
under the sky. Look, how the lawn proceeds

toward my flower garden to hide the boot prints
made the rainy day I plant my white hyacinths,
violets, and a pair of sapling lilacs in the clay.
I offer mulch to encircle this plot and seed

this trench of footsteps to enclose my garden.
The wild of my lawn has met the garden edge,
and hyacinths bow their blooms as though they
lead me in prayer. How long ago my grandfather

would have mowed my lawn. I see him now ride
row by row over the molehills just beneath the sod,
his Gravely tractor the color and smell of rust.
He bounces in his sulky seat, grooms the uneven

texture of the grass smooth. A lawn is a polished place.
I notice in a plot half-cut, a certain palette—the stem
of the grass closest earth and unsunned swells pastel,
but the high grass grows green. What can these shades

changing in the sun mean? Grass is not a lawn
until my grandfather makes it one. He recalls
that I at three stand waist-high to grass and hay
in his back lot, more gold than green there. I hold

a wildflower to my face. By this unkempt moment,
he remembers me, my untamed gesture. A flower
touches my lips and nose. He maintains his lawn,
my youth, has no regard for how the hours pass,

a wristwatch unwound and unmoving, a pair of shadows
lengthen across our faces. I stand in sunshine at midday,
uncut, unbowed, his wildflower. The hay has its season,
so he mows—he mows because this is how one grows.

Composite Magdalene

Dear Mary, mother of all women,
you and I are one. I hear the wheeze

in the joint of your jaw as you gasp
in surprise. A body we share bleeds

so plants around us wither and die.
We dim bright mirrors, we rust iron.

You and I write a monster to life.
In rumors, I am a communist spy.

For treason, another Mary bids me die.
Simply, isn't one woman every woman?

The gospel is a book of Marys, women
who washed Jesus' feet with their tears

and perfume and their hair. Unbelievable,
at the tomb you'll find us Marys there.

Sovereign Mary of Magdalene, I name
our seven demons: self-deprecation,

distracted driving, self-doubt, temper,
jealousy, comments that emasculate

a man. Saints now, penitent women,
we fold our hands to pray, a masquerade.

Bloody Mary, call forward another Mary:
in water she floats with a rope at her waist,

she conceals a mole, a birthmark, a scar—
she's a witch, my dear Mary, we all are.

Compass

Nobody told me to move on.
I made my own compass,
a sewing needle afloat in kerosene.
And I carry my compass with me as I go.
It wavers right and left, west and east of north,
then settles at last on the pole.

At times north is nothing but a point of reference,
a direction to walk away from,
the place from whence one departs.

A part of me, some small part, grieves to leave.
If life begins it must end. One arrives then proceeds.
One carries on.

I take with me my reasons.
A sudden change of mood.
The question: don't you trust me?
Silence at the table. Silence as a question.
Silence as an answer.

At times, magnetic poles can shift.
Last lifetime, perhaps the needle dipped east.
Perhaps the shift itself is a gift,
a merciful reversal of fate.
Still, my mind noses toward how things might have gone.
Carry on, carry on. I have my compass.

Follow Out the Happiest Story

It is evening, and we are two hikers
overnight in the White Mountains.
The season keeps its cycle, never-ending
river where water falls over water
over waterfalls into another river.

Sharp, the scent of evergreen boughs.
Moonlight sticks where pine pitch drips
down and down slow toward deep roots.
Our boots rest there, too, our feet bare
below fleece blankets. We will wait
a little longer to share our secret:
that dying is not quite death, goodnight
is not quite goodbye. Our bodies apart,
two corpses in cloth coffins, after life.

Yet summer breeze sways these two cribs,
our hammocks lined with sleeping bags.

Creation of Eve / Sleep of Adam

My ribcage should blossom soon.
I wait the long hours of an afternoon

for blooms. I imagine soul within skin,
a housecat that hides behind a curtain

on the windowsill with the dust. Flowers
in body seem more reasonable. Peonies,

I think pink peonies, petals soft as feathers,
downy flowers will bud soon with sun.

The bones of my ribcage articulate to one
another under my skin, hidden roots

that have yet to produce. I wait for symbol,
for my bones to reduce. Another Adam and Eve,

you gave a rib to me. If love is our Eden,
a paradise, why am I alone? A peony petal,

a single rib, he loves me, he loves me
not. In your sleep, you bleed, I bloom.

See the deep roots, my petals spread,
invert their curves. Tell me I am beautiful.

View from Highway 46

Parallels, lines together file in fibers
of carpet I clean. I vacuum, imagine
myself from outside this living room,
behind bow windows, behind the iron

bars of our front porch—I share space
with a vacuum, a dustpan and broom.
I clean, but as you return, I leave, you
and I, two commuters in opposing

traffic. I break from my chore to visit
the grocery store, in time to shift out
without signal—escape or accident?
A clean getaway. I survey the room,

empty of company, full of mail, dust
and dirt across hallway. More parallels
exist here than porch rails. Consider
balcony bars and their careful symmetry,

the precision of a prison fence, stiff crib
walls, a ribcage for you and a ribcage
for me. I drive the vacuum with, against
the carpet grains. Between lines appears

a daydream—I drive down a one-lane
highway. The noonday sun grinds clouds
down to a powder lighter than airbag dust
gusted into the air. Two kinds of lines

even here—yellow and white; one double,
dotted, and one unbroken. When I drive,
I align myself with the static white side,
where there is room to turn wide right,

where asphalt fades to gravel or guardrail.
Here I am, I ride closer, close to the other
line, to the other side. I cross the constant
line and the unreliable one—what a way

to die, in someone else's windshield, to die
while I clean opposing lanes into carpet,
to die in the confines of my own mind,
to die an accident in my own daydream.

Situation Comedy

After four episodes of Friends, I sleep.
My podcast says I might be stressed.
I run the dishwasher, after testing

the limit of what I can fit in it,
four pans, two pots, all handles
down. Another limit to understand—

in a dream I stand shovel in hand
over a hole in beach sand. Awake,
I run at seven each morning. I run

to the grocery store, to the bank,
to the gas station, to the bank again.
My podcast guesses I'm depressed.

In the bay of my garage, boxes float,
rowboats in a harbor. A television stand
is a ferry, the spare couch a yacht.

Always one episode of Frasier later,
sleep, dream of a deeper hole, this time
I stand inside to dig. My podcast guesses

I'll listen to a TED Talk about death.
I learn less laundry and more often,
small and smaller cycles. After Seinfeld,

try sleep. Dear Podcast, what will it mean
if the next time I dream of digging, I pile
dirt past my knees, or thighs, or higher?

A Family Portrait, or From Daughter to Father

for N.W.

My business is the train, and I time its rails
each night. The cargo came on the quarter,
and the passenger arrives at nine, rides
over the line of eleven pennies I tape

to the rail. I make the train make me jewelry.
And I am an expert now, this is my superior
product, which, contrary to what you say,
is neither shoddy nor shit. Here, look at this,

Father, on one side of my coin, the outline
of another father—one who will support me
as I support myself. And with one penny see
what I create: this charm for fifteen dollars,

a stamped pendant for ten, and in blank copper
I can beat any name. After labor with aluminum
hammers and stamps, each special penny returns
the affection I invest. This is my craft, dear Father,

my investment. And here is the story I tell as I sell
my pennies: when the train approaches, the coins
would throw themselves far away from the rail.
But the tape preserves their posture, keeps each

penny face-down on the track when the train rides
unaware across its back. Violent, I know, even so
the ends justify the means. After a pearl, the oyster
holds no grudge against a grain of sand. Can you see

the blank coin in my hand? Now see what I see—
this opportunity, beauty. Father, you are the train, you
press away your likeness from the coin of my soul.
And I am a bright, blank, glistening thing.

From Boughs

Cherry blossoms float from their perilous
heights. I bow toward them, a flower girl
back-to-bride to reap petals from the aisle,

a maid drawing a pail from a well. One petal
by petal by pale petal by blushing pale petal—
five to each flower, one for every sense

by which I encounter you, five to the hand
of Fatima, Miriam, five for the Hierophant
on his throne between pillars of liberty

and law, the keys to heaven cherry blossoms
at his feet. Here is the rebellion he assays—
I am Miriam, prophetess of water. I receive

Moses from the Nile, I dance across the dry
Red Sea. My love, I pour out kindness, water
from a cup. Saturate yourself. I am Miriam, leper.

My skin flakes, falls to the ground as though I,
another cherry tree, release blossoms with petals
five, each a face of Shiva, a wound of Christ,

a consonant harmony. My love, I am a girl
in a blue dress, balancing in a wooden bucket
the weight of water from our well, my love.

Thresholds: Maple Street, February

This is a threshold of liminal space, however rare,
what's shared in ending, in beginning, a warm
winter day at the edge of the gallery of nature.

Bare legs, bare head, on a blue mountain bike
over black asphalt, I am riding to visit a brother,
my brief exhibition in the curated space.

Among Maple Street's dense pines, snowbanks
withdraw under late sun, brown and white piles
now reflective pools, wells to receive souls ready.

My rear tire, a wet quill, dips into their inks,
signs my spine. How strange, a warm day in dead
February, apparitions of snow melted to drops

on tree branches shine like funereal pearls. Small
rodents rise, stand up from their burrows to life
again. In their second coming, in the widening road

they die by dawn. Currents of evening air alternate,
tell my body air is water—one of nature's illusions.
I ride through air the sunlight spoiled, stagnant

bathtub water my bare legs wade in their pedaling
steady, and air the snow kept long frozen—each pool
another glass of water thrown into my face to thrill

my skin and fill my lungs. The sun sets further.
Truth or illusion—air holds water, air is water,
condenses, rises above snow piles or falls visible

from air now. How far until the river where a soul
floats free? Air and water rise—imagine the place
where they meet, shadow in the corner of the eye.

Return to Sender

At the end of my driveway, on the left, lonely
as a radio tower, the mailbox transmits no news
from you. Low-frequency waves convey

through the box's black the presence of grocery
store coupons and bank statements. For a single
stamp, count forty-six cents, to mailbox and back,

count forty-five steps, including the turn halfway.
A storm delivers a bank of snow. I sort this ice
with a bare hand. Stamp prices drop, I alone

this century lose money, wait for your letter, your note.
Passive, I observe a plow blade reap the mailbox.
Tunnel-top lands headfirst in the ditch, wooden post

rests across the curb, and the red semaphore flag
arrives on starched-white driveway ice, a bright
schoolyard nosebleed. I mail my letters nowhere.

I write again, again. I kneel below *La Mort de Marat,*
pray to patron saint of post, post scriptum, postpartum.
This is the Zodiac speaking: the letter is a silent art.

Leap

for M.G. and C.P.

Black water as always, but low
for September. Along the rocks
the shore retreats from the water,

now pollen bands like tree rings
display the age of drought. Stones
shine, broken glass. Under my feet,

a boulder radiates noonday heat,
poises me over pond, patient, waits
for me to leap. Minnows, clouds

in schools crowd the tops of trees
to the western shore. And I rock,
a boat tied loose to a dock, prepare

myself to launch at water. A breeze
against bare skin reminds me fall
approaches. Sunlight sails over water

behind the wind, beams on waves
so its sheen mirrors scales of a fish.
I will jump soon. I recall Whetstone

Pond, then, when I cannot jump I cry.
My father by my life vest casts me in,
his swift skipping stone. I fear fall

and fauna, crayfish floating to wire
traps. Once I jumped, but I have fallen
older, my soul swims against my body,

its mesh coils. Now who will seize me?
Who throws me in? Still above Davis
Pond, I see the public pool twelve-feet

deep, and the boulder, my headstone,
another rigid Dover Y diving board,
never gives. Take a breath. That dive

was years ago, that dive is every day.
So now life, timeless deep dive. I wait
to leap, ready to leap, leap—I rise

from the water. Eyes open to graffiti
on the boulder's side. At eye-level
in red and white, a submarine.

Dishes by Hand, Sleight of Hand

Our kitchen sink has two sides,
a natural divide. I rinse dishes
in either half, cast uneven shadows

on the backsplash. Shapes of bowl
and spatulas attach to white tiles.
A black rabbit appears in our sink,

a magician's bottomless black hat.
Your dishes, my dishes, together
in the basin. Warm water, soap suds

the sponge. Our sink has two sides,
not all do, but I like to think in twos,
dirty and clean, empty and full, question

and answer. You keep roses, scarves,
a deck of cards hidden at your wrist.
Another pair, magician and assistant.

Your trick—I wash your dishes. I hear
that others wash plates by the basin,
baptize knife by knife their cutlery

in pools of water and soap. Saucers,
spoons, immerse, emerge, by the water
cleaned. Do not seek redemption here.

A blade disappears, halves crate and woman.
I fear the knife beneath the surface.
When I wash your dirty dishes, I rinse.

Woman, Wellside

The rain washes away any memory
the front lawn kept of the winter—
a kind of forgetting by the garden shed.
A drift of snow thaws, almost bronze
at the edges, unhides a gold locket bright
in the sun. Near the second garage bay,
a yellow plow, that abandoned friend
of a friend. The darkest season passes
as April pours itself out—not a decay
but a displacement—culverts swell
into canals. A wishing well unsatisfied,
memory surges, chemicals shape
and change the brain. Darkness collects
water and my coins, copper pieces
I release for my ritual wish.

Head of a Woman

In memory, we share one room, perfumed
by lavender blooms, a bed on the floor, one

blanket. You weave lavender in my hair, sew
blossoms into bedsheets, cross-stitch buds

into pillowcase. Pale yellow thread and needle
samplers chant *lavare, lavare,* to wash, to wash.

Turn the card, six cups, each of purple flowers
full. *Where there is lavender there is love,* says

one who was loved. The windowsill collects
a single honeybee looking for lavender to stave

its black plague. It returns with drops of honey,
gold coins with the mark of its queen. Deconstruct

a memory and what is gained? Even there, love
remains either solid or void. What I recall is either

a tray I fill with foreign currency, clean linen,
and pressed flowers or a window that reaches

infinitely back. Memory is a field of broken glass,
a mirror shatters in half, in half, in half. No fragment

overcomes the whole, a memory incomplete. Drowsy
from lavender oil, I love you as light through a prism.

Mother Murders Marion Crane

On the bathroom floor, dark clothes over white
tiles. Behind a gold curtain, a plastic one;
translucent, it transmutes the steam that rises

to skylight. The mirror frames my form, waits
for fog. I avert my eyes. A towel for sheepskin,
I model Eve in this bathroom, my private Eden,

embarrassed by my own breasts. A shower scene
in impressionist style: I look through my nudity
not at it, distort what form I recognize in outline

of pelvic bone or line of shoulder to shoulder
art unattainable. Unclean, unclean, unclean, calls
the water stream. Penitence—in my confessional,

the porcelain walls force a certain discourse, exact
from the body a holiness the body cannot bare.
Honey, or the synthetic scent of something sweet,

in humid air drifts. Just once, couldn't I be Venus
with her distant stare? Our emotional reticence
presents as emptiness. Gentle as it is, my gentle

conditioner teases my eyes, but no tears. I stand
in the half-shell of my tub, face to the porcelain,
place the spout to my back. Between what's in,

what's out, one strikes a careful balance. Conditioner
retreats with shampoo, coils the drain eventually.
I share the sin of all women: nudity signifies divinity.

If I approve my bare reflection, I cast my own idol.
Here acceptance, my own golden calf, grows
from what I am willing to sacrifice, my modesty,

an heirloom from my mother and her mother, too.
I melt it down in this crucible, my comfort rises
as dross. I, the idolater, know the price exacted

of the one who tolerates her own bare body: in a cup
she receives back that acceptance ground to powder.
Punished, she drinks until that cup is clean, clean,

clean. Long light lavender strokes conceal blank body.
No artist paints me. I paint myself. The canvas lays
stiff, a corpse, but the mirror remains ever animate.

Nudity demands divinity not dignity. Venus uncovers
her other bare breast to wave her hand at the emperor
who commissioned the scene. He stands clothed

in invisible robes. I bend to shave my legs, imitate
the upright shave's unstable pose, propaganda's flat
affect. Adolescent, I am a girl unprepared for razor.

It carves long red lines behind the crease of my knee
and into my shin. Still, the razor cuts me. Naked,
I bleed and bleed. I am oil and acrylic on fabric,

I am marble, and I am an older woman now, she prays
not to fall in her shower, not to die, unclothed, alone.
Clean, I emerge and swaddle myself in cotton to dry.

Open Graves in Spring

A mausoleum looms like a cottage
on the cemetery lawn. Behind, a forest
stretches wide as a yawn, prepares
to swallow stone by stone the wall
and the path leading from road to gate.
To the tomb, this cemetery is a next-door
neighbor. Rain arrives in early spring.
The dead emerge from within earth,
chauffeured in coffins for a garden party.
Two ravens play croquet with the ribcage
of a stranger. An owl, like a prince, scolds
a peasant to his skull. The scavengers,
foxes and coyotes in aprons of fur, sweep
away the clutter, keep the lawn from disorder.
And the land rises again from the grave.

Subject / Object

      You cannot know what I wear under my clothes.
Last night I posed nude from the waist up, in side-profile
a real Renaissance woman. My breasts bare, yet I coiled
a snake
              at my neck, a charm I borrowed from my dear
Cleopatra,
     and isn't it weird? It is unclear whether my choker
invokes the asp of wisdom or the sign of original sin.

             A personal detail, overshared.
Eyes closed still, imagine the damp wall of a cave, or a public
bathroom stall, or the Sistine ceiling, or a rubber mud flap—
any flat space
     makes a canvas for a woman's body. Here is my body
spoken for you, and here is a hospital room, late Friday
     though early in May—my birth or death?

     In the shopping mall, where clothes make a woman,
swimsuit season and a shell game:
                        the silver thimble keeps a pearl;
the walnut shell, a stone smooth as a razor-shaved leg; the conch
shell, my wedding band;
     but the bombshell shelters my virginity.
                             Wear clothes, make
a woman. A secret: beneath this dress throbs Lady Macbeth.

Clotho, Lachesis, Atropos

for M.M. and V.P.

In time, unruly hair plays tame; it grows, no matter how slow.
Keeping time, we cut. I pinch and twist my hair. We weave

our hair in and out of rooms, tapestry threads across ancient
loom. Before this bathroom mirror, I trim bangs between dull

scissor blades. I measure my passing time in strands of hair,
elsewhere another sweeps the floor to keep her time. I trim—

hair retains no memory of why it's cut; I trim—one strand,
a lifeline thread holds together past, future, present. She and I,

second Sampson and Delilah, discover every blade has two sides,
cut with scissors and permission. And there, a woman without hair,

by chance or choice? This woman braids, Medusa with her crown
of snakes, their molting skins flake at her feet. Teach me to dread

the mirror before I turn to stone. Who am I to cut my own hair? This
woman saves a lock of hair in a locket, as if she could fasten

time behind gold hinges safe. And here, a strand of white spins
from distaff to spindle, is measured by rod, lays against blade.

Better Homes and Gardens

Inside the calmest eye of hurricane, we talk
of weather. Hello, the sun is out again. Wind
and pressure shift to drive inside spiders, ants,

and other insects. The weather orders their lives,
the weather scaffolds our platitudes. Frogs croak
from the lagoon, signal rain, monsoon. A spider

climbs the white sides of my tub. I do not drown
the spider, but I do not pick it up. No, I trap it
in a cup until the lack of air kills, not me. So ends

our friendship. How are you? Dew is on the grass,
rain will not come to pass. Rain three days, I want
us over quickly, abandoning any blame. Drawers,

doors all stick before rain. I introduce myself again.
Won't you ask me how I am? A spider's touch
remains long after the arachnid has gone. You feel

it too? At my ankles and wrists its touch persists.
The weather doesn't change. I have nothing left
to say. Still, I wonder this—if the winds reverse,

if I find you trapped like that spider inside my tub,
and you cannot flee my empty glass, will you learn
opposing pressures grow a cyclone? Within the eye

air sinks, blue sky silences violent wind. But winds
reverse, blame shifts, the eyewall's edge intensifies.
You are the spider, I the weather forcing you inside

to die. I clean my empty tub, set aside a special glass.
Another Noah to test the depths after a deluge,
I release spiders like white doves from my stoop.

Sum

He dies on Thursday
night. Time pins us

here. In leaves, gusts,
and torrents, the gems

of windshield invigorate
smoke, coronate, suspend.

Other drivers travel on,
ignore this passing. Skid

lines mark pendulums across
Elm Street. The station wagon

casts its transmission forty feet
behind, into a graveyard wall,

of all places. To draw back
that moment forty years, to store

its energy back five minutes:
arrows quiver against bows,

await archers. Stationary, a star
occupies a space, a moment.

Light through a prism—now
he is, and now he will be.

The release—now he was,
now he is not.

Death, a Hall of Mirrors

Any place death makes a grave.
A grave follows its own strict rules,
the measurements of a casket, a row
of headstones, a roadside cross. But
death refracts a person, that last
hall of mirrors with its many edges
each sharper than the guillotine.
Each reflection is a false image.

When I pass beyond my last reflection,
I pray to find a field of white wildflowers.

So the Sadness Could Not Hurt

> *Somewhere in him, a shadow turned mournfully over.*
> *You had to run with a night like this so the sadness could not hurt.*
> —Ray Bradbury, *Something Wicked This Way Comes*

By now, it is difficult to discover any beauty
in the world, or any left who believe in it.

Under the Ferris wheel where I pause,
all signs and wonders point to a twilight

in midsummer, cusp of daylight preceding
a solstice's short night. Elsewhere, dough

rises and awaits its powder. Cotton candy
clouds crowd out one another, sticky storms.

The main thing is: about time and eternity,
about heaven, I retain my doubts. On wooden

tracks cascades a rollercoaster, sharp corner,
the final car snaps, whip at the end of its crack.

Slicing bright, a slight burn, fluorescent lights
glow long, trapped gasses press into my vision,

temporary cataracts. What here is not intended
to distract? If I am a disciple, I am she who asks

to be asked to demonstrate her belief. Credit me
with my miracle. Carousel music plays away,

a tinkling ring clear in cooling air. Somewhere joy
and terror share their space—shrieks catch in far

corners of a haunted house, curl away from the backs
of cars twirling clockwise on their sides, silk webs

split. This carnival where marquee lights and rides
surge in tempestuous waves is no place to wonder

at the length of days, or at the ways I learned a person
might pray to believe—she tosses a coin to wishing well,

she turns a stranger's face on a playing card.
Beside me, balloons swell against their strings,

each a kite eager to rise into the sky. A Ferris wheel
carriage arrives, Christ inside. At his tattered sneakers,

I empty my pockets. The contents: a set of keys,
plastic tokens, a ticket stub torn in two, the fortune

Zoltan promised me in the penny arcade. We rise
with the ride, a compass where no needle stirs

for I have arrived. Iridescent lights on the backs
and sides of park rides glow, unfading as the face

of Christ. A red balloon escapes its tether, rises
beside us, higher. Dear Ruth, I write this down

for you: Christ calls us by another secret name,
this is the answer. This is the last coin, the lost one.

About the Author

Ruth Towne is the author of *Resurrection of the Mannequins* (Kelsay Books, 2025). She is a graduate of the University of Southern Maine's Stonecoast MFA.

Her poetry has appeared in *Holy Gossip, The Lily Poetry Review, Decadent Review, New Feathers Anthology, Coffin Bell Journal, New Note Poetry, In Parentheses,* and the *Stonecoast Review*'s Staff Spotlight. Her poetry has also appeared in Stanford's *Mantis: A Journal of Poetry, Criticism, and Translation.* Her poem "So the Sadness Could Not Hurt" received the second-place Grantchester Award from *The Orchards Poetry Journal.* Her poem "S@lv@d°r D@l!'s Mannequin," published in *BAM Quarterly,* Issue III, was nominated for the 2025 Best of the Net Anthology.

www.ingramcontent.com/pod-product-compliance
Lightning Source LLC
Chambersburg PA
CBHW030916170426
43193CB00009BA/873